a
little book
for

Lovers

a
little book
for
Lovers

GEORG FEUERSTEIN

SOUNDS TRUE

Sounds True, Inc.
Boulder CO 80306

© 2006 by Georg Feuerstein
All rights reserved. Originally published in 1996
under the pseudonym Dana Goodwin.

Printed in Canada

ISBN: 1-59179-471-4

Feuerstein, Georg.
      A Little Book for Lovers.

Library of Congress Control Number: 2006923917

This book is dedicated to all lovers who see
the great Mystery in the eyes of their beloved.

Grateful acknowledgment is made to
Dr. Caroline Phillips for her
valuable editorial assistance.

Contents

Preface

Love escapes definition. It is as ineffable as light or life. Sexual love, too, bursts the boundaries of language. Whenever anyone says sex is such and such, do not be fooled. Any explanation is necessarily partial. And even numerous partial explanations do not make a whole. Certainly, no answer makes or breaks a mystery. And our lives in all their myriad aspects are embedded in and held by a great Mystery.

That Mystery pulsates in the distant galaxies as much as it throbs in the human body and sparkles in the delight of sexual play.

Thus this little book will not tell you precisely what sexual love is. It will offer you no more than helpful pointers. It will evoke potent images, suggest possibilities, and hint at ways of sensing the all-pervading Mystery.

Our sexuality, like our breathing and thinking and doing, wells up in the inexhaustible Mystery of existence. And as we begin to feel that Mystery, our spiritual heart burgeons and our body starts to sing. The song that wells forth in our sexuality is as beautiful as it is ancient. It is the song of Life itself.

We are all familiar with the song of Life. We are all eager to hear it, to receive it in our body, and to thrill at its inherent joy. Yet sometimes we forget its soothing, enlivening existence and our longing for its harmonies. Then we become lost in the dark labyrinth of unhappiness. Once we are thus lost, we needlessly toil to recover the joyous song that ever reverberates in the chambers of our own heart.

May you and I always be mindful of this joyous song.

Georg Feuerstein

part one

LOVE &
OTHER
VIRTUES

1

Mystery's Hidden Song

Do not assume that sex is two bodies in friction, producing merely pleasurable sensations. This error is perpetuated by those who have lost touch with the Mystery of life. Stimulation of the senses only yields a trickle of pleasure. It can never be a portal to happiness or bliss.

The senses hurl us into the outer world where we might become easily lost. They scatter our consciousness and dispel the beauty of our inner unity. They are common thieves who rob us of harmony and throw us off balance, tricksters who pretend to give us everything but who leave us nothing. The senses fragment our world, dazzling our mind with glittering pieces of no ultimate value. Even as we reach out to grasp fragment after fragment, the promised satisfaction evaporates, causing us unhappiness and restless hankering.

The Mystery thrives only when the clamorous senses are pacified. There can be no vivifying song when mouths clutch each other hungrily, without quietly abiding in the moment. Our heart's soft song escapes those who desperately push on to the next bodily sensation, until all is spent in a single cataclysmic discharge of life.

The rhythmic slamming of bodies drowns out the gentle melody that is forever pulsing at the heart. The heart delights in motionless silence. It closes its petals at the sight of blindly grasping hands that knead only flesh but feel not the Spirit's crystal texture.

Mystery cannot thrive in noise. It is born of stillness. Noise repels the Spirit, which manifests only in the presence of harmony.

The jagged sounds of sense-bound sexing are a sure citadel against the Spirit. When the heart thumps furiously from greedy exertion, its echoing beat drowns out the Spirit's everlasting song, which inheres and continuously creates the filaments of space and time.

Only when the body is in balance and the mind is freed from the turmoil of the grasping senses can the eternal song emerge at the heart and work its magic in our life. We hear that song only through the wisdom of intimacy, which severs the bond of mere sensory pleasure. ♠

2

Intimacy: Breaking the Wall

Mystery's song is a golden gift of intimacy and love.

Our world has forgotten how to be intimate. Everywhere people think that intimacy is a matter of much talk and more action. But this yields only an illusion of intimacy. We can be together without hearing and seeing one another, without *being* with each other.

Even if our bodies squeeze tightly against each other, we may not feel anything beyond skin touching skin. Our bodies can be formidable castles, allowing no feelings in or out. But it is through feeling that we connect to other beings in a human way. Sensation, rather than feeling, belongs to the realm of matter. But feeling is the language of the heart.

Feeling is the bedrock of intimacy. Without feeling, we are incapable of reaching outside our protective shell. Without feeling, we are not even able to reach within ourselves for the precious truths hidden in our innermost being. Without feeling, we are dead. And how many today have abandoned feeling out of fear, despair, and ignorance?

Many are strangers to themselves. How can they hope to be intimate with another being? We cannot bridge the apparent gap between ourselves and others as long as we have not found access to the secret chamber of our own inner being. We must become intimate with ourselves: we must know and love ourselves first before we can truly love and enjoy the fullness of intimacy with another being.

Those entombed in their own feelingless existence do not know the joy of intimacy. Instead they suffer their self-imposed prison of

aloneness. They do not know that the same Life
is present in all of us and that, casting all fear
aside, we can find ourselves in the mirror of the
other being: he or she meets us halfway in our
quest for self-understanding and intimacy.

At last, we can discover ourselves as the Life
that lives *through* and *as* the other being just as
it lives through and as us.

Intimacy melts down the high walls erected by
our fears, hurts, and disappointments. It allows
us to discover that we are not alone. It connects
across the gulf between that which is within
and that which is without. It removes our ill-
fated illusion of being abandoned and restores

unity where previously duality governed our perceptions and intentions.

Through intimacy we create an opening in our sequestered existence, permitting Life to flow abundantly into us and out of us into the other person and the world. Intimacy shows us that all along we ourselves created our isolation and loneliness.

Intimacy halves our experience of sorrow and pain, the inevitable companions of finite existence. And it magnifies our experience of joy. Through joy the vicissitudes of human existence become bearable and ultimately meaningful.

As we learn to trust Life, intimacy becomes easier. Gradually we are able to widen our circle of feeling to include more and more beings, both human and nonhuman, until we are able to open our arms to the whole cosmos in ecstatic communion. For ecstasy is the ultimate degree of intimacy, in which nothing is excluded from our embrace.

True intimacy is the great silent expanse in which recognition and love arise. When we are truly intimate with someone, there is no separation. Distance does not matter. Space is rolled in on itself. Time stands still. We simply *are.* And we *are together* with the other being, mutually disarmed and vulnerable.

Intimacy is transplanting oneself into the all-embracing Mystery of the other. Then when we reach out to touch, it is not only our skin that makes contact, but our whole being extends itself to include the other and to be included in the other's being. The boundaries we habitually erect around ourselves fade away as a puff of smoke. Thus intimacy is a form of meltdown in which our core is exposed to the other. ♠

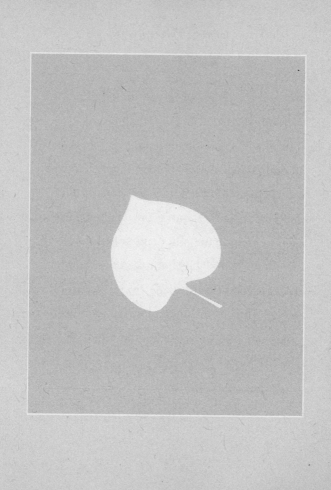

3

Vulnerability: The Art of
Being Wounded

Vulnerability is the womb that gives birth to love. Vulnerability is woundedness. The vulnerable person carries a subtle wound in her heart. The wound is caused by her contact with the callousness of the world—the fact that flowers wilt, rocks turn to sand, and human body-minds age and die; the fact that we own nothing and that everything we call ours is merely on loan to us; the fact that our fellow beings all too often choose lovelessness and withholding over concern and self-sharing; that fact that we are so easily strangers to ourselves; and the fact that even when we try to embrace others we are prone to hurt rather than uplift, punish rather than forgive.

Vulnerability is living without masks. The vulnerable person voluntarily abandons his walls of self-protection and permits the world to impinge on his psyche as it may. He does not seek pain for pain's sake, but he cultivates vulnerability so that his heart may not harden to the pain of others and to the shock of universal

death. She lives vulnerably because in her
openness she finds strength, beauty, and love.
What is more, her woundedness keeps her
mindful of her true nature, which lies beyond
pain and pleasure, life and death.

In the eyes of the world, such vulnerability
is as outmoded as the virtue of humility. More
than outmoded, both virtues have become an
unspoken taboo in our secular, self-serving
civilization. The vulnerable person is deemed
foolish, and the humble person is secretly
shunned as a loser or a fake. Both are an
embarrassment to the ego-ensconced individual
whose existence revolves around furthering his

or her own cause, while being immune to the delight and pain of others.

Invulnerability is itself a form of arrogance, since it implicitly denies the value of others. The ego is an epiphany of unlove. Such unlove is more than the absence of love; it actively undermines love.

The ego is inherently proud, tolerating no lord or law above itself. Its natural inclination is to inflate itself. In humility, this intrinsic propensity of the ego is checked. The humble person puts herself above no one, for she has understood that all beings arise within the same

Being and that, ultimately, none is inferior and none superior. ♠

4

Loving Is All-Inclusive

To be capable of true intimacy and true vulnerability is to love. But what is love? It cannot be defined but merely circumscribed. Love is not a forced promise or a sentimental memento. Love grows out of intimacy. For love to be genuine it must become as vast as space and time itself.

Love is not a noun. Rather it is *to be* loving, now and now and now. Love is not a thought, not even an intention. It is a state of being, which is always in a process of completion. Lovers are people who have stepped outside the angry world of kept and broken promises, of expectations and disappointments, of need and hurt.

Lovers are people in whom the tree of the great Mystery comes to fruition, its fruit ripening as compassion and charity.

When we love, feeling Life's pulse in the other is easy. When we love, giving of ourselves is natural. Love is of the essence of participation. Unlove is exclusion in body and in mind. As love spreads its warm glow through and beyond our being, it pulls us out of all inertia and insularity. We become cosmopolitans. We taste our affinity with everyone and everything, and we delight in it.

Love is truly blind. It contains no judgment, only unconditional affirmation of our own being and the being of others. In truth, love is so blind that it does not recognize any otherness. Its embrace is all-inclusive. ♠

5

Compassion Is Vulnerable Love in Action

Like love, compassion is a state of being, not a state of mind. And so is charity. By means of both we step across the threshold of our individual existence, beyond the microcosm of our human personality, beyond the wall of our skin. Through compassion and charity love is rendered tangible. Both are great ecological powers, completing the circle of being.

Compassion is the vulnerable, open heart that flows out to the other, because there is understanding and love. In compassion, we acknowledge the other as being worthy of our regard, affirmation, and loving support. Compassion is the inevitable gesture of healing the rift that separates one individual from another.

Compassion is possible because, as loving beings, we have understood that everyone's embodiment is always threatened with pain and extinction. We share the same fate with everyone else, and our love enables us to confess our own suffering and mortality, as

well as our fundamental fear of death. This
makes us vulnerable and sensitive to the fear
and suffering of others.

In our love and compassion, we rise
victoriously beyond anxiety and uncertainty,
and affirm the all-inclusive Being itself. But
this affirmation is not abstract. Compassion
must be as concrete as the individual to
whom it is directed, who is always to be seen
as a manifestation of Being, of the great
Mystery of existence. ♠

6

Charity Is a Form of Union

W hen we love, compassion and charity come effortlessly to us. They are love's exhalation. Genuine love is ever blessing. Selfish love can easily be recognized, for it dilates itself in pleasant words and easy gestures, while withholding the great gifts of compassion and charity.

Charity is the vulnerable, open hand that unceasingly reaches out to the other, across the apparent gulf of fear that disunites individuals from each other and from the rest of the world. In charity, we affirm our fundamental oneness with everyone. In charity, we acknowledge the other as being worthy of our self-sacrifice.

Charity is incessant self-giving, based not on pity but on wisdom and compassion. Through wisdom, charity is made viable. For indiscriminate charity has no transformative power and can even do harm. Through compassion, charity is removed from snobbish do-gooding. Without compassion, charity can easily sink into calculated self-interest.

True charity ennobles the other person. The art of selfless giving provides the recipient with the opportunity to participate more fully in life. It enhances his existence. It vivifies her.

Through charity, we celebrate our unity in the circle of Being. Our charitable acts are forms of joyous union, in which donor and recipient acknowledge their common source.

How many times, through countless ages, have we both given and received? ♠

7

Embodied Love

Genuine love is always incarnate. We cannot love with our ideas. For love to be love it needs the body—our breath and our senses. It needs another incarnate being. It needs the body of the world. Such love is inherently erotic. Eros is the affirmation of Being in all its multifarious forms. It is not otherworldly. It is not tidy

and timid. It is a consuming passion. Love is
the wildly beating heart of the cosmos itself.
Remember, the cosmos is the eternal body of
the ultimate Being.

In the mystery of sex, we can hear the
luminous heart, which for infinite eons pumps
the blood of life to nourish all the cells of
cosmic existence.

Love, like sex and life, surpasses the mind.
You cannot will yourself to love another. Love
is hidden in every fiber of the body. It remains
hidden as long as thought erects its walls. But
love, which rises of its own accord, can break
down even those mind-made fortifications by

which we surround ourselves and seek to make
ourselves invulnerable.

Although you cannot force love to appear,
you can invite it into your heart and life. You
can soften your edges so that love may blossom
within you. And when it does, you can hold
it there — not by force but by your continued
willingness to let go of fear, anger, envy,
jealousy, greed, and all other negative emotions
and attitudes.

Love is like the fairy-tale princess, who could
not waken from her slumber until gently kissed.
The prince's gentle kiss dispels the terrible
magic that has kept her banished from the

living. Gentleness is of the same family as love, just as "gentle" and "gentile" belong together and originally meant "belonging to the same clan." Gentleness is a harbinger of love.

You can learn to be gentle, and thus let down the drawbridge to your castle. Gentleness is a form of openness, which fills your body with vibrant energy. On the wings of that energy rides love. So long as you incarcerate yourself in your lonely castle, you will hunger for love. The absence of love is a pain that gnaws at you, whether you admit it or not. If you do not love, you will always long for love. All your thoughts and actions will carry the same message: "Love me!" "Love only me!" "Love me completely!" "Love me unconditionally!"

Yet this need for love will never be fulfilled. No one, however much he or she may love you, can remedy your own lovelessness. No number of assurances and kisses can restore love to your heart. You will always ask for more. You will beg and demand. You will even try to trick others into loving you.

But all your ploys to call forth love in your life are doomed to fail because love cannot enter your life from without. The prince is already in the castle with you. Love is present in you even now. But it is invisible to you because you look to others for love.

Love comes to those who are ready *to love* rather than merely *to be loved*. The prince of the fairy tale was in love with the princess even before he set eyes on her. He sought her out, endured great hardship, and fought off all kinds of dangers long before he was able to hold her beautiful face in his hands. What sustained him was his budding love for her.

You always only seek that of which you are already aware. You are looking for love because, deep down, you know that it exists. Your only error is that you have fixed your gaze on externals, while the key to love lies in your own heart.

Those virtues, like compassion and charity, that come spontaneously when you love can be cultivated long before love has taken firm residence in your heart.

Tread gently, then, on the path of life! ♠

part two

THE
MYSTERY
of the
LOVER

8

You Cannot Know Your Lover

D o not assume you know who your lover is. Such knowledge breeds contempt. And contempt creates distance and unlove. Do not confuse your lover with the person who has this or that name, shape, age, background, or mannerisms, or about whom you could tell a hundred sad or funny stories. Your lover is not merely that. He is not exhausted by all these

characteristics. She is not defined by any of the
qualities you could list about her.

Accept your lover as a great mystery—as *the*
Mystery. Your lover is not a stranger. Neither
is he or she familiar. Yet you will desire to
know your lover, to understand him entirely,
to penetrate all her secrets. This impulse is
destined to be frustrated. For, the knowing mind
always bounces off the Mystery.

When you think you know your lover, you
only know your mind's own forms. Your lover
is an inexhaustible fullness that can never be
completely known. It is your impatience that
spawns the illusion of familiarity.

But your impulse to know your lover also harbors, however imperceptibly, a genuine desire—to merge with him, to become utterly one with her. Such merging or oneness is beyond all knowledge, just as it is beyond all manifest forms. It occurs in the intangible Mystery itself. The impulse to know everything about your lover is only a perversion of that deep-felt desire for oneness.

Look into your lover's eyes, and what you see is a vast Mystery. New lovers sense this. But all too often they are looking for themselves in the other. When they gaze into each other's eyes, they merely find their own baffling excitement

47

and appetites. They do not gaze deep enough. They look but do not see. ❧

9

The Folly of Romantic Love

Lacking wisdom, people confuse romance with love. Even so, their love—however immature—is infinitely preferable to the ossified hearts of those who have traded vulnerability for cynicism.

But romance, too, is self-centered and self-indulgent. Even as the romantic lover worships his beloved, he only worships himself. Even as she dotingly caresses his every breath and word, she only idolizes her own desires and hopes.

Romantic love is therefore destined to erode under the impact of the merciless wind of time. People fall in love, and they fall out of love. Genuine love, however, is about rising rather than falling. When you truly love, you are uplifted; you are lifted beyond your ordinary self, even beyond time. And you uplift your beloved as well. Such love alone is lasting. Such love alone is fulfilling. Such love alone is bliss.

How many times have you fallen in love? How often have you thought it was the love of your life only to be disappointed later?

Genuine love is not to be found below, requiring you to fall down into it. It is not for a brief span of time, not even for one short lifetime only. Rather it is eternal. It is the perennial Reality, which cannot be romance, inveigled, idolized, or compressed into any personal scheme. It forever escapes the ego.

Romantic love is a magic spell woven by the ego that feels unloved and desires to be loved. Hence lovers always try to makes themselves desirable. It is the body they adore, sometimes perhaps the mind, but never the soul. Yet romantic lovers are prone to borrow the soul's language or their self-possessed declarations of

eternal love. Unknowingly they betray the soul
and stifle the Spirit's spark. For they are merely
bewitched by desire.

When we look closely, romantic love is the
melodrama of unlove. It is of the ego and hence
can never reach across space and time to delight
in the other's true being.

Only in genuine love, which is free from
all idealization, are the ego's distortions of
truth overcome.

Romantic love is exaggerated and thus it
makes a travesty out of the poesy that is true
love. True love cannot be caricatured because
its features are universal, not peculiar to

any limited human personality, however charming or attractive. True love exceeds the ego infinitely. ❧

10

Your Lover Is a Blazing Radiance

What do you see when you gaze deeply into your lover's eyes? *Who* do you see? *Who* is gazing back at you? The answer is simple: the very Mystery that is also you.

Do not reduce your lover to the person whose smile sets your heart aflutter or whose gentle, knowing touch stirs you deep within. Do not confuse your lover with the person whose lips

fill your every cell with a compelling hunger
and who succeeds in shattering all your reasons
with a single glance. Your lover is not the other
with whom you lie entwined, limbs melting
with limbs.

Your lover is the Beloved by whom and in whom
all—both lovers and those failing to love—are
forever embraced. The Beloved is the action of
limitless love, of timeless ecstasy. He/She is ever
close to all things and incessantly whispers in our
ears. He/She is the One spoken of by the world's
lovers of wisdom, worshipped by the great religious
teachers, and longed for by those who have grown
weary of their isolation and unhappiness.

Your lover is a blazing radiance.

How could you possibly confine him to your pictures of him, or your hopes and fears? You will never succeed in shaping her to your desires. Your lover is *all* lovers, resonant with love.

Your lover is the Ancient One from whom all love pours forth into the world. He is unspeakably blissful. She is a miracle of boundless ecstasy. Your lover is truly worthy of worship. Bow down to the Beloved. Raise your face and receive the light of grace. ❧

part three

WALKING
upon the
RAINBOW
of LOVE

11

The Birth of Love in Stillness

Love rises from the waters of tranquility, when the mind's cares are suspended and thoughts do not trouble the body. To walk on the path of love, you must cultivate quietude—stillness of the body and stillness of the mind.

Render your body as still as the lunar orb drifting slowly across a cloudless sky at night. It shines with a borrowed light, as does the human mind and body.

The Life that animates you comes from a place far beyond the grasp of your hands and far beyond the reach of the thoughts. As you silence the many voices resounding in your bodily being, that all-giving Life pulsates more strongly in you. As you put to rest the turmoil of your thoughts, that Life is mirrored more brightly, more faithfully, by your mind.

Unless you immerse yourself deeply in that Life, you cannot hear its subtle song, and your ears will be filled with the disquieting cacophony of the world.

Wherever you are, sit then quite motionless within and without. Remember the palpable stillness of the great mountains of this Earth. They simply abide in timeless meditation, patiently witnessing the passing of the seasons and ages. Even a raging storm cannot diminish their tranquility, and their peaks are forever bathed in pure sunlight.

When you sit motionless and undisturbed, you are grounded and unshakeable like a mountain. And with your inner sense reaching up, you begin to touch the golden light of the Mystery and hear its sparkling song. 🌱

12

The Breath of Life

As you rejoice more and more in the stillness of the body and mind, you begin to notice a deepening of the breath. The breath connects you to Life, to the cosmos, to your lover.

Understand and observe that you are not the one who is doing the breathing. The breath flows of its own accord, just as thoughts spontaneously bubble up in our consciousness.

At first, you will find that the flow of your breath is shallow and erratic, like water from a downpour looking for its destination and tracing a crisscross pattern in the soil.

You will discover with dismay that the rhythm of your breathing is interrupted by thoughts and feelings that suddenly jump like frogs into your field of awareness. Gradually, however, it evens out.

The breath comes from beyond you—a messenger from infinity. On its steady current rides tranquility and strength of purpose. It connects you with every other being in the universe. Breath is the vehicle by which your

innermost essence, the Spirit, shines forth in
the body and the mind. It unites you; it makes
you one; it makes you whole. Your inhalation
is the universe's exhalation. When you exhale,
the cosmos inhales. You breathe together,
in rhythm.

The breath carries you beyond the narrow limits
of the body; it streams through the boundaries
set up by the mind. You are truly permeable, and
the breath is the all-pervading force entering and
leaving your body-mind, which is only a diminutive
local structure in the stupendous universe.

Breathing simply happens, just as thinking
simply happens. We cannot claim to do either.

Both breath and thought arise of their own accord out of the silent Mystery.

Even though you can give direction to your thinking, the thoughts pop into existence by themselves. Even the greatest thinker is subject to this necessary spontaneity.

When we allow ourselves to feel the vast peace in which we are continuously immersed, we seem to become still. Then we breathe more deeply, too.

Abide in stillness with your beloved.

Let the breath flow out and into your beloved and receive your lover's breath into you.

Witness that the space between you is alive. Feel it. Feel how the breath reaches across that silent expanse, filling it with Life and strength.

Your lover is the cosmos that breathes you. You are united through the breath—the most natural way of self-sharing.

We breathe together with billions of other living beings. We share the same breath. We participate in the same substance that is transmitted through the breath. We are all tied together in a living tapestry through the breath. All those connections are present in your lover.

What mystery! ✿

13

Cultivating the True Center

Center yourself. Withdraw from the outer ripples of your existence and focus on your innermost being. At the periphery is no stillness, no bliss — only constant change and uncertainty. Wholeness is at the center. Stillness is there, and inexpressible delight.

Our senses are forever flying toward objects. This centrifugal tendency of the body makes us inwardly restless. We must find our true center. The eye of the storm is calm.

Your center coincides with the center of your beloved. It coincides with the center of all beings, and of the cosmos itself.

At the center we are all joined in holy stillness. This is the kiss of Being. At the center, the fierce storm that howls at the periphery remains insignificant, a distant occurrence of little consequence.

Allow your lover's breath to travel freely across the space between you. In receiving her breath, you receive the Life within her. Let her breath center you further. Receive his breath, which

will warm your being and place you at the heart
of all things.

Feel the breath. Do not merely listen to
the rushing of air into your nostrils. Listen
beyond it to the soundless song that forever
fills all space.

Your lover's breath is a supreme gift—the
gift of Life. It comes straight from the timeless
domain of the Spirit.

Permit your own breath to well up deep
within you, and allow it to flow through you to
your lover. Let it carry your message of love.

At the center of your being is the wellspring of
Life, which is ever harmonious and blissful.

When the breath of Life is awake in you and your beloved, reach across the living space to join hands. Allow the breath to travel along your arms, to and fro, until the boundaries dissolve still more. Who is touching whom? Who is seated opposite whom? Distinctions become blurred when the hard edges of the ego are absent. The ego bows out when the breath grows strong.

14

Closing the Circle of Ecstasy

As soon as the ego abdicates, Life can flow freely and abundantly *in, through,* and *as* us. Then unalloyed joy spreads through every fiber of our being. Then we vibrate in unison with our beloved and with all beings and things.

This is the eternal moment of ecstasy—not the end of our journey but the strong seed of ultimate transformation. In ecstasy, we

discover our true nature by whose light we
can illumine and ennoble every aspect of our
existence. Such enlightenment, sustained by
wisdom and compassion, must become our
means of continued self-transformation and
self-transcendence. Henceforth all our thoughts,
words, and deeds must be purified and fortified
in the fire of ecstasy. In this way we may be
present in this world as a blessing for all beings.
All beings are our beloved, and we approach
and serve them with wise compassion.

The task of enlightenment is endless. The
need for compassionate action is also endless.
But nourished in ecstasy by the breath of Life

itself, we are able to persist in our self-chosen obligation to lighten the burden of others.

Through ecstasy, time stands revealed as a powerless illusion. Only Life exists. Only the Beloved in the form of all beings and things exists. Thus our light and delight know no bounds. We are the Whole—a dance of happiness and love. ❦

15

You Are the Luminous Beloved

When you recognize the Beloved in your lover, when there is only a single breath between you and your lover, all movement is a harmony of light.

Light is the Source. Light is the immortal substance out of which you, your lover, and every other being and thing is fashioned. Light is the means by

which we return to the Source. Light is
our destination.

This light has no cause. It is self-luminous
and all-illuminating. Past, present, and future
are encapsulated within it. Outside it, nothing
can ever exist. The Light has no extension
and no velocity. All things are instantaneously
coexistent in it. All things are created and
supported by it.

This supernal Light is utmost delight,
illimitable bliss. Behold your lover in the
supernal rainbow of delight. He is perfect
stillness, filled with the fullness of Life. She
is perfect motion, devoid of any loss. There is

both deepest knowing and utter astonishment. There is wisdom and wonder. For you and your lover are a miracle occurring in the everlasting Now.

In his eyes the glimmering galaxies whirl endlessly through time. In her eyes time gathers itself into a delicate bouquet of all past moments and all future destines.

In the fullness of this vision there is only the One, who sees and is seen, who hears and is heard, who arises as all things and in whom all things arise.

Now the world in its totality stands unconcealed: a translucent weave of mind-spun possibilities stretched simultaneously over the infinity of joy. It is seen to be a relic of memory, as evanescent as a bubble.

The shimmering colors of time and the flimsy forms of space are recognized as temporary playful appearances that pop into and blink out of existence without warning. They are random manifestations within the unfathomable singular Being. They have no *ultimate* significance. Only the enduring One has meaning beyond measure. For the One is absolutely free, untainted by limitation. It is the perfection of desire, and the absence of want. It is unthreatened perpetual existence.

But that One is continuously rendering itself tangible in the multitude of forms. It is forever disclosing its beauty, radiance, and joy in all beings and things. To behold this eternal truth, we merely must open our hearts to that which is never withheld from us.

Rejoice! Rejoice! Rejoice!

There is only the Beloved, who is infinite love. There is only the Beloved, who is you.

There is only the Beloved. 🍂

In the beginning was the One.
In the present is the One.
In the end will be the One.

The One is fullness.
The One is emptiness.
The One is neither fullness
nor emptiness.

To say "One" is to utter
one word too many.

About the Author

Georg Feuerstein, Ph.D., is counted among the leading voices of the East/West dialogue and since the late 1960s has made many significant contributions to our understanding of India's spiritual heritage, notably Hindu Yoga.

He has authored more than thirty books, including the award-winning *The Shambhala Encyclopedia of Yoga, The Yoga Tradition,*

Sacred Sexuality, Lucid Waking, Tantra: Path of Ecstasy, Holy Madness, The Mystery of Light, and *Structures of Consciousness.* His most recent books are *Yoga Morality* and *Aha! Reflections on the Meaning of Everything.*

His distance-learning courses on the philosophy and history of Yoga and on Classical Yoga are available through Traditional Yoga Studies (www.traditionalyogastudies.com).

He is a practitioner of Tibetan Buddhist Yoga and resides in Canada.

SOUNDS TRUE was founded with a clear vision: to disseminate spiritual wisdom. Located in Boulder, Colorado, Sounds True publishes teaching programs that are designed to educate, uplift, and inspire. With more than 550 titles available, we work with many of the leading spiritual teachers, thinkers, healers, and visionary artists of our time.

For a free catalog please contact Sounds True via the World Wide Web at www.soundstrue.com, call us toll free at 800-333-9185, or write:

The Sounds True Catalog
PO Box 8010
Boulder CO 80306